HELEN OXENBURY

Tiny Tim

Verses for Children

Chosen by Jill Bennett

Heinemann: London

For Simon and Sarah

William Heinemann Ltd
10 Upper Grosvenor Street, London W1X 9PA
LONDON MELBOURNE
AUCKLAND JOHANNESBURG

This selection © Jill Bennett 1981
Illustrations © Helen Oxenbury 1981
434 95601 5

Printed in Hong Kong by Wing King Tong Co Ltd
Reprinted 1983, 1984, 1987

Acknowledgements
The compiler, illustrator and publishers would like to thank the following for permission to reproduce the poems in this book:
Atheneum Publishers for "The Owl" by Conrad Aiken from *Cats and Bats and Things with Wings: Poems by Conrad Aiken* published by Atheneum, © 1965 by Conrad Aiken; E P Dutton for "Jump and Giggle" by Evelyn Beyer from *Another Here and Now Story Book* by Lucy Sprague Mitchell, copyright 1937 by E P Dutton & Co. Inc. Renewal copyright 1965 by Lucy Sprague Mitchell; Macmillan Publishers Ltd for "I saw a jolly hunter" from *Figgie Hobbin* by Charles Causley; A E Dudley for "Grandma Gurney"; The Society of Authors as the literary representative of Rose Fyleman, and Doubleday and Co. Inc., for "Mice"; William Jay Smith for "The Toaster" from *Laughing time*, published by Atlantic-Little, Brown, 1955, copyright © 1955 by William Jay Smith; James Kirkup for "There was an Old Man" from *Round About Nine* published by Frederick Warne Ltd; Macmillan Publishing Co. Inc. for "The Little Turtle" from *Golden Wheels* by Vachel Lindsay, copyright 1920 by Macmillan Publishing Co. Inc., renewed 1948 by Elizabeth C Lindsay; Oxford University Press for "A Pig Tale" from *The Blackbird in the Lilac* by James Reeves, publishing by Oxford University Press, 1952; Andre Deutsch Ltd for "Down behind the Dustbin" from *Mind Your Own Business* by Michael Rosen; A & C Black (Publishers) Ltd for "The Engine Driver" by Clive Sansom from *Speech Rhymes*; Sidgwick & Jackson Ltd for "Choosing Shoes" from *The Very Thing* by Ffrida Wolfe.

One-eyed Jack, the pirate chief,
Was a terrible, fearsome ocean thief.
He wore a peg
Upon one leg;
He wore a hook –
And a dirty look!
One-eyed Jack, the pirate chief –
A terrible, fearsome ocean thief!

ANON.

New shoes, new shoes,
Red and pink and blue shoes,
Tell me what would *you* choose
If they'd let us buy?

Buckle shoes, bow shoes,
Pretty pointy-toe shoes,
Strappy, cappy low shoes;
Let's have some to try.

Bright shoes, white shoes,
Dandy dance-by-night shoes,
Perhaps-a-little-tight shoes;
Like some? So would I.

BUT

Flat shoes, fat shoes,
Stump-along-like-that shoes,
Wipe-them-on-the-mat shoes
O that's the sort they'll buy.

FFRIDA WOLFE

A silver-scaled dragon
             with jaws flaming red
Sits at my elbow and toasts my bread.
I hand him fat slices,
             and then, one by one,
He hands them back
             when he sees they are done.

WILLIAM JAY SMITH

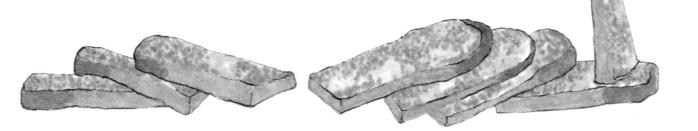

There was a little turtle.
He lived in a box.
He swam in a puddle.
He climbed on the rocks.

He snapped at a mosquito.
He snapped at a flea.
He snapped at a minnow.
And he snapped at me.

He caught the mosquito.
He caught the flea.
He caught the minnow.
But he didn't catch me.

VACHEL LINDSAY

The train goes running along the line,
Jicketty-can, jicketty-can.
I wish it were mine, I wish it were mine,
Jicketty-can, jicketty-can.
The engine driver stands in front,
He makes it run, he makes it shunt;

Out of the town,
Out of the town,
Over the hill,
Over the down,
Under the bridges,
Across the lea,
Over the ridge
And down to the sea,
With a jicketty-can, jicketty-can,
Jicketty-jicketty-jicketty-can,
Jicketty-can, jicketty-can.

CLIVE SANSOM

I had a little brother
His name was Tiny Tim
I put him in the bathtub
To teach him how to swim
He drank up all the water
He ate up all the soap
He died last night
With a bubble in his throat

In came the doctor
In came the nurse
In came the lady
With the alligator purse
Dead said the doctor
Dead said the nurse
Dead said the lady
With the alligator purse
Out went the doctor
Out went the nurse
Out went the lady
With the alligator purse.

ANON.

Billy is blowing his trumpet;
Bertie is banging a tin;
Betty is crying for Mummy
And Bob has pricked Ben with a pin.
Baby is crying out loudly;
He's out on the lawn in his pram.
I am the only one silent
And I've eaten all of the jam.

ANON.

Algy met a bear,
A bear met Algy.

The bear was bulgy,
The bulge was Algy.

ANON.

Poor Jane Higgins,
She had five piggins,
And one got drowned in the Irish Sea.

Poor Jane Higgins,
She had four piggins,
And one flew over a sycamore tree.

Poor Jane Higgins,
She had three piggins
And one was taken away for pork.

Poor Jane Higgins,
She had two piggins,
And one was sent to the Bishop of Cork.

Poor Jane Higgins,
She had one piggin,
And that was struck by a shower of hail,

So poor Jane Higgins,
She had no piggins,
And that's the end of my little pig tale.

JAMES REEVES

Down behind the dustbin
I met a dog called Jim.
He didn't know me
and I didn't know him.

MICHAEL ROSEN

There was an old man
Had a face made of cake
He stuck it with currants
And put it in to bake.

The oven was hot,
He baked it too much,
It came out covered
With a crunchy crust.

The eyes went pop,
The currants went bang,
And that was the end
Of that old man.

JAMES KIRKUP

Five little monkeys walked along the shore;

One went a-sailing,

Then there were four.

Four little monkeys climbed up a tree;

One of them tumbled down,

Then there were three.

Three little monkeys found a pot of glue;

One got stuck in it,

Then there were two.

Two little monkeys found a currant bun;

One ran away with it,

Then there was one.

One little monkey cried all afternoon,

So they put him in an aeroplane

And sent him to the moon.

ANON.

Frogs jump
Caterpillars hump

Worms wiggle
Bugs jiggle

Rabbits hop
Horses clop

Snakes slide
Sea-gulls glide

Mice creep
Deer leap

Puppies bounce
Kittens pounce

Lions stalk –
But –
I *walk!*

EVELYN BEYER

Greedy little sparrow,
  Great big crow,
Saucy little tomtits
  All in a row.

Are you very hungry,
  No place to go?
Come and eat my breadcrumbs,
  In the snow.

ANON.

In the dark, dark wood, there was
   a dark, dark house,
And in that dark, dark house, there was
   a dark, dark room,
And in that dark, dark room, there was
   a dark, dark cupboard,
And in that dark, dark cupboard, there was
   a dark, dark shelf,
And on that dark, dark shelf, there was
   a dark, dark box,
And in that dark, dark box, there was a...

GHOST!

ANON.

I saw a jolly hunter
With a jolly gun
Walking in the country
In the jolly sun.

In the jolly meadow
Sat a jolly hare.
Saw the jolly hunter.
Took jolly care.

Hunter jolly eager –
Sight of jolly prey.
Forgot gun pointing
Wrong jolly way.

Jolly hunter jolly head
Over heels gone.
Jolly old safety-catch
Not jolly on.

Bang went the jolly gun.
Hunter jolly dead.
Jolly hare got clean away.
Jolly good, I said.

CHARLES CAUSLEY

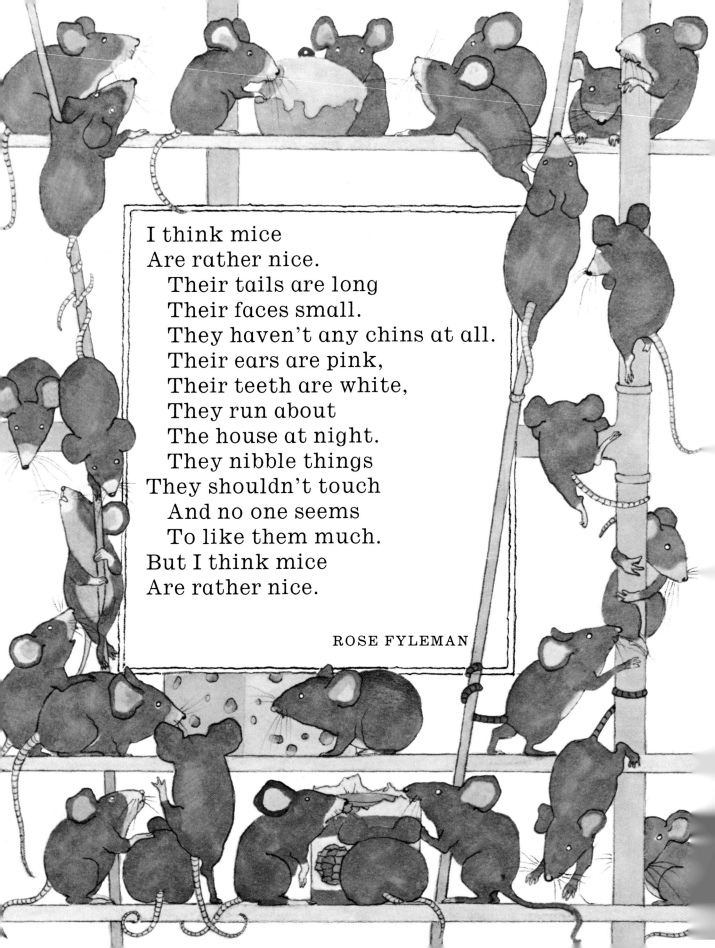

I think mice
Are rather nice.
   Their tails are long
   Their faces small.
   They haven't any chins at all.
   Their ears are pink,
   Their teeth are white,
   They run about
   The house at night.
   They nibble things
They shouldn't touch
   And no one seems
   To like them much.
But I think mice
Are rather nice.

ROSE FYLEMAN

To whit
to whoo
he stares
right through
whatever
he looks at
maybe
YOU
and so
whatever
else
you do
don't
   ever
      ever
        be
          a
           mouse
        or
       if
     you
are
   STAY
     IN
       YOUR
        HOUSE

CONRAD AIKEN

Grandma Gurney
Gives to me
Gooseberry tart
And hot sweet tea.

She sits up high
On her rocking chair.
She can't touch the floor
But she doesn't care.

Grandma Gurney
Is tiny and grey.
I wonder if
She'll shrink away?

Grandma Gurney
Has grown very small.
One day she won't be
There at all.

A. E. DUDLEY

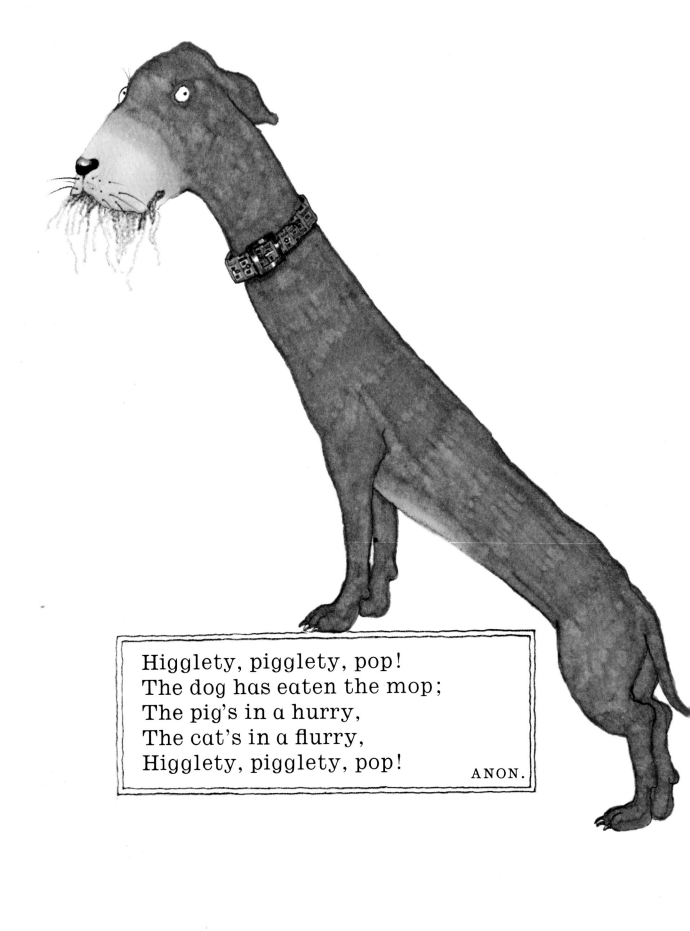

Higglety, pigglety, pop!
The dog has eaten the mop;
The pig's in a hurry,
The cat's in a flurry,
Higglety, pigglety, pop!

ANON.